BLIND CHESS

with

RANDY J PHIFER

RJP MOTIVATION

Stimulate the mind and the brain without pieces nor board

Build self-confidence

Promote practical problem solving

Wise decision making

Exhilaration and exciting

Enhance intellectual strategic thinking

Strengthen short-term memory

Copyright © 2015 Randy J Phifer
All rights reserved
First Edition

PAGE PUBLISHING, INC.
New York, NY

First originally published by Page Publishing, Inc. 2015

ISBN 978-1-68139-549-4 (pbk)
ISBN 978-1-68139-550-0 (digital)

Printed in the United States of America

THE EVOLUTION

As an athlete, the competitive spirit followed me with every sport played whether handball, base-ball, basketball, football, table tennis, etc. Chess is no exception.

Chess has been influential and significant in my life ever since my father taught me how to play at eight years old. The most contributive and life-benefiting lesson I've learned is that even if you lose a major piece, like sight, you can still win the game. The game strategically relates to everyday life in many ways.

The love I had for my father was immense, so merely spending time playing chess with him was an amazing pleasure. If he loved me, he didn't show it by letting me win. As a matter of fact, I waited exhaustingly until I was sixteen years old to finally win my first game against him. Although at that time, I was handily beating most of the opponents I faced.

In the early years, only a few of my friends and relatives even played chess strategically. When I was in junior high school, two brothers (Charlie and Butch) moved in my apartment building. They were older than me and were very good chess players. Many times we would play well into the wee hours of the morning. New York City is the city where chess players never sleep. About that time, I also began working in Manhattan as a messenger and courier. The great thing about that job was it afforded me the opportunity to occasionally stop in the park and kibitz or play a game of chess. Manhattan has many parks with stone tables that have chess boards built in as well as benches where opponents can just play chess. All you have to bring are the pieces. I really miss that. Nevertheless, my performance caliber increased exponentially. In addition to that, in 1972, Bobby Fisher and Boris Spassky (both chess grand masters) played World Chess Championship 1972 that was televised and analyzed. Studying that game raised my strategic skill, finally propelling me to victory over my father. Hooray! Amazingly, my father never ever won another game against me after that. From there I went on to play for my high school and college. More recently, I've enjoyed Wednesday evening chess with the same Overland Park friends for nearly twenty years.

Along the way, diabetic retinopathy rendered me totally blind, challenging my chess future. To not have the ability to see the board nor the pieces posed a tremendous problem. I sadly feared chess was over. For two unbearably long years, I was without chess although I thought of it constantly. A tremendous void existed, particularly since my father had risen to glory and was now playing angelic chess in heaven.

My reflections of my father's tutelage led me to revisit life strategies, such as should your little brother want to leave and journey across the dangerous and threatening street, an older, wiser, and stronger person must watch over and supervise him. Similarly so, when a pawn or lesser-value piece is released, it too must be protected. Life experiences emphasize structure, preparation, and organization, which also keenly parallel chess strategies. At the Rehabilitation Center for the Blind and Visually Impaired in Topeka, Professor Schmitt, the braille instructor, introduced me to tactile chess. That's where the board resembles a pegboard and each of the sixty-four squares can receive a single piece with a peg that inserts into the hole. It allows the recognition and handling of the pieces and board formation. Thank God, chess was back in my life. Neuropathy is yet another personal affliction that I endure. It makes it difficult to accurately pick the pieces up and place them back down in the hole, which is most frustrating. Therefore, I learned and perfected calling out the piece and move, not touching the board at all. Algebraic notation is the method and process used to identify each move made. The majority of the games I play these days are over the phone, where my opponent handles the board on their end, tells me their move, and I merely inform them of my move response. I'm not as good as I once was, but I've retained a relatively high caliber of play and still achieve a respectable number of victories. For opponents to suffer chess defeat seems abusive and difficult enough, but to lose to a blind man who neither sees nor touches the board may justify their eligibility for psychotherapy. The memory is greatly enhanced by Blind Chess. My cousin and I were playing over the phone, engaged in a very good game. At that time, I fortuitously forked his king and queen. All of a sudden I hear a bang. My cousin informed me that his dog accidently knocked over the board, and we will need to start over. Confidently I responded, "Au contraire, cousin, I remember where every piece was and it ultimately resulted in victory ." The agony of defeat om chess is very serious. I call this technique and style, Blind Chess. Blind chess stimulates the mind, builds self-confidence, promotes practical problem solving and wise decision making. It's exhilarating and exciting. It enhances intellectual strategic thinking and strengthens short-term memory. These qualities will definitely benefit and delight many aspects of your life. Learn Blind Chess and grant me the distinct privilege and honor of teaching you.

BLIND CHESS

PLAYING RECOMMENDATIONS

The motivational and inspirational method in teaching the game of Blind Chess using no tangible boards or pieces enhances and benefits your overall life.

BLIND CHESS

THE CONCEPT

Stimulate the Mind and Exercise the Brain using neither board nor pieces.

Chess is a game that challenges the mind with strategy. Blind chess transforms the tangible chess game exclusively to the mind, eliminating the board and pieces. The intricate and complex strategies are formulated in the mind in direct combat against the opponent. Blind chess exercises the brain as one would exercise any muscle. All of the situations that can occur in chess can be easily translated and related to everyday life, making it more familiar than you could ever imagine.

Build Self-Confidence

To understand and play chess appears a daunting task to many. Like learning the alphabet in stages, one can not only understand it but become proficient in it. Once you learn this game, the innumerable possibilities become apparent to you. To expand the chess game exclusively to the mind develops a powerful confidence of accomplishment and rewarding self-esteem.

Promote Practical Problem Solving

There are often several solutions to a problem. Each solution can rectify the inherent problem at hand. For instance, logically, many words can be used to satisfy a sentence. There are many ways to play the game and solve the problem at hand.

Wise Decision Making

Unlike mere practical problem solving, some intense and complex problems require certain resolutions. Where several words can satisfy a sentence, often only one word can absolutely nail it. With chess strategies, given the a specific requirement, the decision maker can then make a resolution after considering all the variable and ending with a conclusion that will inform the decision to be made.

Exhilarating and Exciting

When mentally playing Blind Chess, with your successful strategies, you either win a battle or you win the game. That feeling of success and accomplishment can only be paralleled to hitting a home run, making a three-point shot, or scoring a goal. To win a game mind to mind can result in a euphoria equivalent to winning a championship.

Enhance Intellectual Strategic Thinking

In order to play the game successfully, one must combine a series of strategic and complex battles. The intellect of your opponent will generate a higher level of response on your part, avoiding as many mistakes as possible. The degree of effectiveness executed in chess strategies can be directly related to the thinking process of everyday life. It will encourage you to process strategies at a higher caliber.

Strengthen Short-term Memory

Remembering how the board is set up, the location of the pieces, including pieces that are revealed when one is moved, and the process of studying strategic possibilities offers a magnificent mental exercise. Maintaining all of this mental activity is difficult; therefore, concentration and practicing empathy and leniency is imperative.

HISTORY OF CHESS

The history of chess spans some 1,500 years. The earliest predecessors of the game originated in India, prior to the sixth century AD. From India, the game spread to Persia. When the Arabs conquered Persia, chess was taken up by the Muslim world and subsequently, through the Moorish conquest of Hispania, spread to Southern Europe. In Europe, the game evolved into its current form in the fifteenth century. In the second half of the nineteenth century, modern tournament play began, and the first world chess championship was held in 1886. The twentieth century saw great leaps forward in chess theory and the establishment of the World Chess Federation (FIDE). Developments in the twenty-first century include the employment of computers for analysis, team consultations, and online gaming.

The earliest precursor of modern chess is a game called *chaturanga*, which flourished in India during the sixth century and is the earliest known game to have two essential features found in all later chess variations—different pieces having different powers (which was not the case with checkers and go), and victory depending on the fate of one piece, the king of modern chess. Other game pieces (speculatively called "chess pieces") uncovered in archaeological findings are considered as coming from other, distantly related board games, which may have had boards of one hundred squares or more.

How to Play Blind Chess

Chess is considered an intellectual and very strategic game utilizing serious intensity. Blind Chess extends that level of play and eliminates tangible crutches, like the board and pieces, making it even more difficult. Don't be disillusioned though. Once learned, the game offers exceptional benefits. Patience is key in allowing a strategy to develop. The sense of accomplishment, the shear enjoyment, and the cerebral strengths offered are unparalleled. The actual strategies of chess and Blind Chess are similar. Maintaining everything in your head harbors the difference. The difficulty lies in configuring the actual pieces and board exclusively cerebrally.

White always moves first and starts the attack. From that move on, defense must be considered before any additional attacking move. Remember, there are many ways to attack. Although, only one choice will be considered. Equally so, the opposition has many ways to attack. You must carefully choose his best method of attack and defend it accordingly. Keeping several different attacks and defense possibilities in your head is challenging. The most challenging is returning to the actual last move made. The more you do it, the easier it will become. To respond to a defense with a puissant offense can be considered winning a battle. Not only must you remember all the current battles, you must prioritize and ascertain the hottest situations before your next move. A game-winning strategy can be achieved by capturing a piece or developing a valuable position. Sometimes losing a piece to gain position leads the way to victory. The number of points left on the board is irrelevant, the win is the only thing that counts.

Maintaining all of this mental activity is difficult, therefore, practicing empathy and leniency is imperative. In other words, Blind Chess must equal a gentlemen's game of chess with understanding. Checking the piece formation when it's your turn is highly recommended. Allowing your opponent to take a move back, avoiding a silly mistake is a wonderful attitude to have, and it creates a higher caliber game. This level of leniency is healthy from novice to intermediate play. Most of all enjoy, have fun, and allow the thrill of the game to supersede winning.

ALGEBRAIC NOTATION

Recognizing the Board

First we learn the board formation and its coordinates. The vertical squares or columns, denoted with letters A–H are called file. The horizontal squares or rows, denoted with numbers 1–8, are called rank.

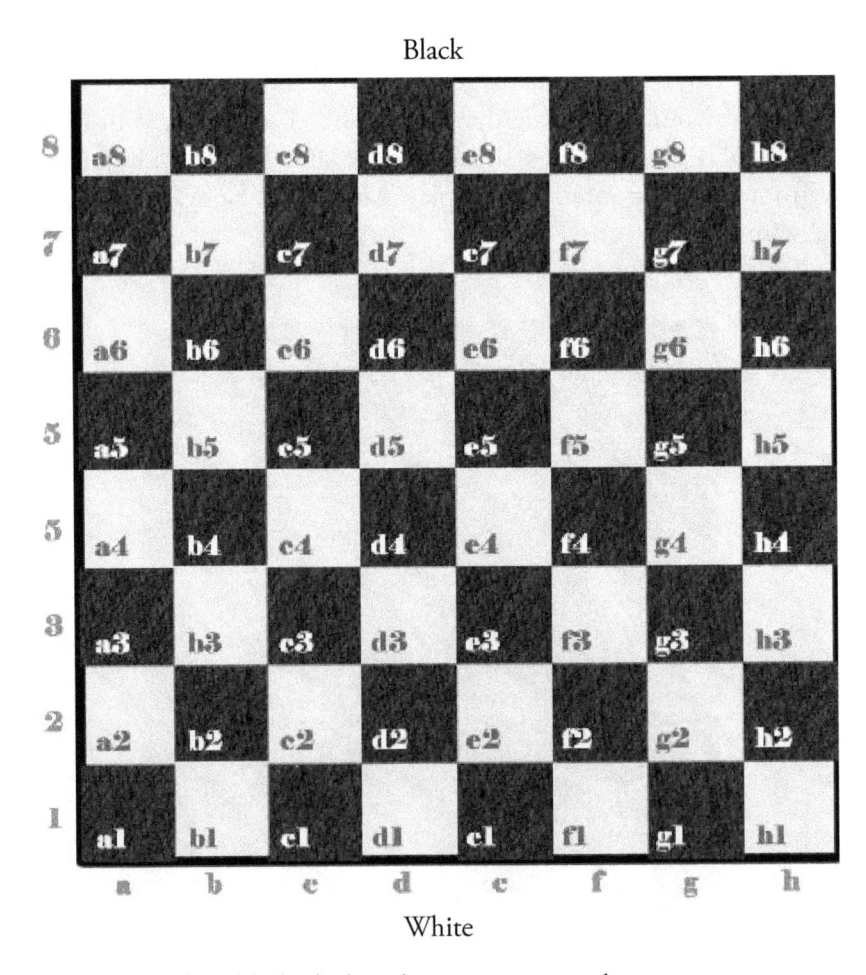

Note: H1 has to be a white square. If it is black, the board is set up incorrectly.

The History

Algebraic notation was developed by Philip Stamma in the early seventeenth century. Stamma used the modern names of the squares, but he used *p* for pawn moves and the original file of a piece (A through H) instead of the initial letter of the piece's name. Although Stamma's version of algebraic notation was created in the seventeenth century, it wasn't widely used until the 1970s. Stamma was born in 1705 in Aleppo, Syria. He was a chess master, helped develop modern chess, and was known for his book *The Noble Game of Chess* in 1745. Algebraic notation replaced descriptive notation, which was created several centuries ago and was used to call the pieces by name.

Starting Chess Position

Black

White

Note: The queen starts out on her color.

* Right White

Notating the Game Moves

Noting the chess moves: You write down your chess move by writing down the number of the move, the piece, and square names of beginning and ending squares. Moves are numbered, and the first move of the game is move 1. After writing down the move number, write down the letter abbreviation for the piece that is moving; the pawn has no letter assigned to it.

White moves are noted in column 1 and black moves are noted in column 2.

Next, write down the square where the piece starts and add the square the piece is going to. For instance, to describe the move of a Knight from its original square (g1) to square f3, writing down 1Ng1. Move number is 1, the N stands for Knight,; g1 stands for the square the Knight was on before the move. Next, add a hyphen (-)., which stands for the word to (1 .Ng1 -__. Next, add the square the piece is moving to, i.e., f3. The move is described as 1.Ng1-f3. In English, for move 1., the Knight moved from g1 to f3.

Date _____ Tournament_____

_____ VS. _____

1.   1.
2.   2.
3.   3.
4.   4.
5.   5.
6.   6.
7.   7.
8.   8.
9.   9.
10.   10.

Date _____ Tournament_____

White   Black

1. f2-f4   e7-e5
2. f4xe5   d7-d6
3. e5xd6   Bf8xd6
4. g2-g3   Qd8-g5
5. Ng1-f3   Qg5xg3+
6. h2xg3   Bd6xg3++

Legend

Piece	Symbol
King	K
Queen	Q
Rook	R
Bishop	B
Knight	N
Pawn	(no symbol)
Capture Move	X
Castling (kingside)	0-0
Castling (queenside)	0-0-0
Check	+
En Passant	EP
Stalemate	
Draw	½ - ½"
Checkmate	#

Note: All definitions can be found in the chess glossary on pages 21-23

King

The King has no numerical value.
The King is the prize. When the King is under attack and cannot avoid that attack, the game is over.
The King moves in every direction, 1 space at a time. That is, it can move along rank, file or diagonal one space.
The only exception is Castling.
The King cannot move within 1 square of the opposing King.

Castling
- King moves to his side or Queen's side 2 squares.
- Rook jumps over King toward middle of the board adjacent to the King.
- All pieces in-between have to have moved.
- It must be the initial move of both the King and the Rook
- Castling cannot occur when the King is in check, he cannot move across a check, and he cannot land on a square that leaves him in check.

Check
- When any piece attacks the King, it demands an immediate response to that threat.
- Check must be announced.
- The King has to move out of Check by capturing or blocking the threatening piece or the King has to move out of the way.

Checkmate
- When a King cannot avoid the attack by the three methods mentioned in check, that is checkmate. At that point, the game is over.

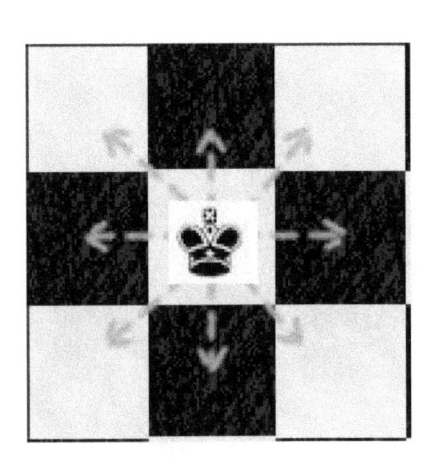

Queen

The Queen has a 9-point value.

The Queen can move in every direction. She has unlimited movement along the rank, file, and diagonal.

When a Queen is being attacked, guarding must be announced except when a Queen attacks an opposing Queen.

Rook

The Rook is valued at 5 points.

The Rook can move unlimited squares on the rank or file.

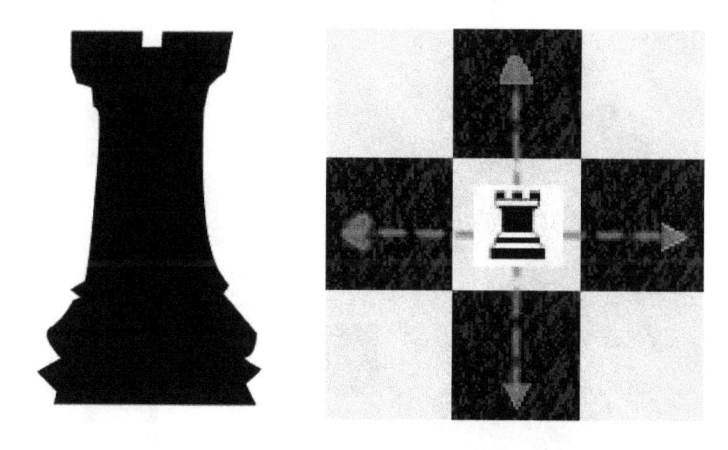

Bishop

It can be used in castling with the king.
The Bishop is valued at 3 points.
The Bishop moves diagonally on its original color.
The Bishop on the white and the black can never land on the same square.

Knight

The Knight is valued at 3 points
The Knight moves two squares on the rank or the file, and one square perpendicular, making the move L-shaped.
The Knight is the only character who can jump over another piece.
It cannot land on its own piece.

Pawn

The pawn is valued at 1 point.
The pawn only moves along the Rank, except when attacking. The Pawn can move initially 1 or w squares and one square thereafter.
The pawn attacks diagonally 1 square.

En passant (French, in passing) pawn is when a pawn initially moves two squares and lands adjacent to an opposing pawn. En passant is optional. In advancing two squares, the pawn passed over a square which the opposing adjacent pawn was attacking. The adjacent opposition pawn may then capture the pawn that originally moved two squares, and advance diagonally to the square that was passed over. The alternative is to ignore en passant, let that position stand, and make another move.

2 Move Checkmate (Fools-mate)

Name___White   Black___Name

1. f3 – e6
2. g4 – Qh4#

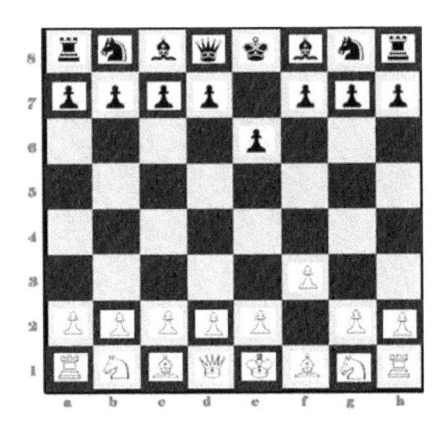

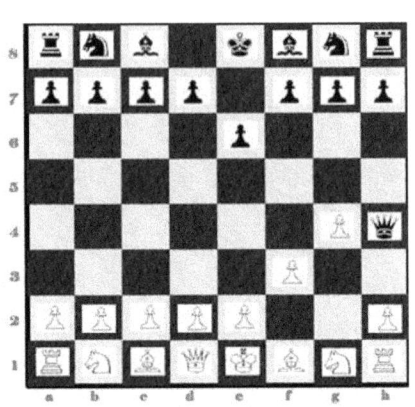

3 Move Knight Checkmate

Name___White   Black___Name

1. e4 – Nc6
2. g3 – Nd4
3. Ne2 – Nf3#

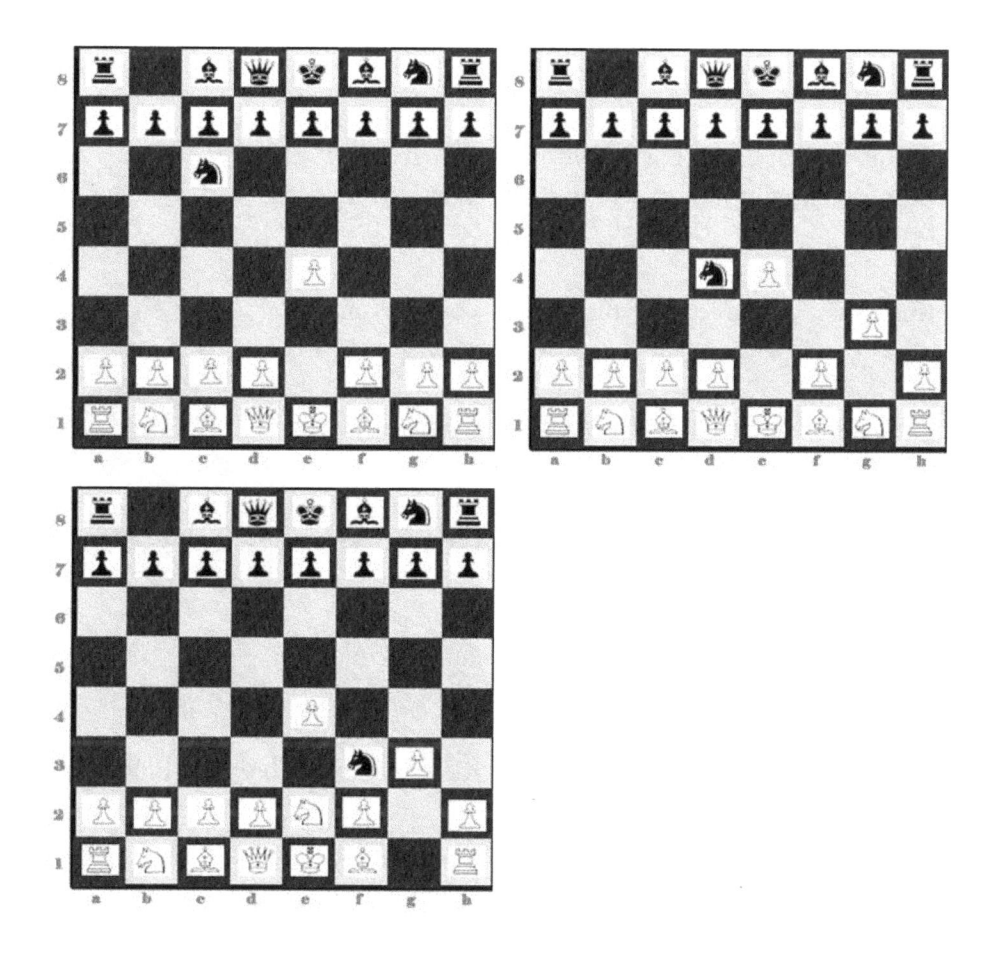

CHESS GLOSSARY

Absolute Pin – A pin against the King called absolute because the pinned piece cannot legally move as it would expose the King to check.

Active – A piece that is able to move to control many squares.

Active defense – The use of attack as a defense rather than passively trying to cover weaknesses.

Alekhine's gun – A formation in which a Queen backs two Rooks on the same file.

Algebraic Notation – Where each square has its name. Rank or Columns of squares are 1–8. The File or Rows are A–H.

Bind – A stranglehold on a position that is difficult for the opponent to break. A bind is usually an advantage in space created by advanced pawns.

Capture – When one piece takes another piece and replaces its position on the board

Castling – Where the King moves on the rank 2 spaces to left or right, shielded by the Rook.

Check – Where the King is under attack.

Checkmate – Where the King cannot maneuver or attack and the game is over.

Center – The D and E files are the center files. The center of the board is of great strategic significance as pieces placed there generally have the greatest scope.

Connected Rooks – When the two Rooks are on the same rank or file with no pieces or Pawns between them. Rooks are very strong when they are connected as they support each other.

Consolidate – Taking care of your position before continuing active operations. This could mean adding protection to critical Pawns or squares, improving the placement of pieces, or making the King safer.

Decoy – The offering of material in order to get an enemy piece to move or the lure of an opponent's piece to a square that is particularly vulnerable.

Draw – A game where neither player wins. See Stalemate for details.

Elo rating – An internationally accepted mathematical system for ranking chess players created by Arpad Elo.

En Passant – When a pawn initially moves two squares and lands adjacent to an opposing pawn, en passant is optional. In advancing two squares, the pawn passed over a square, which the opposing adjacent pawn was attacking. The adjacent opposition pawn may then capture the pawn that originally moved two squares and advance diagonally to the square that was passed over. The alternative is to ignore en passant, let that position stand, and make another move.

Fork – A form of double attack where one piece threatens two enemy pieces at the same time. In a triple fork, three enemy pieces are threatened.

Guarding – When the Queen is under attack by another piece other than the Queen.

Interpose – To place a piece in the path of a check or to block.

Promotion – When a pawn reaches the final rank, it can be turned into another piece (except a Pawn or King), usually into a Queen, also known as "Queening."

Rank and File – Rank are rows of horizontal squares, Left and Right. File are columns, vertical or up and down.

Resign – When a player sees his position is hopeless and ends the game before checkmate.

Skewer – A tactic where an enemy piece is attacked and forced to move, exposing another enemy piece behind it to capture.

Stalemate – Equals a draw where no one wins.

- If your King is not in check, but you can't move without bringing your King into check, the game is over and is considered to be a draw when neither opponent can win.
- When a player decides there is no point in continuing the game because he can't win and might even lose, that player can offer his opponent a draw. If the opponent accepts, the game ends.
- Draw by Insufficient Material. A game is considered to be a draw when one of the following endings occurs:
    - King against King with no other pieces on the board.
    - King against King with only a Bishop and Knight on the board.
    - King and Bishop against King and Bishop, with both the Bishops on diagonals of the same color.

- Draw by the 50-Move Rule. The game is also drawn when at least 50 consecutive moves have been made by each side without any captures or Pawn moves.
- Draw by Three-fold Repetition. This draw comes about if exactly the same board position occurs 3 times, with the same player having the move each time.

Weakness – A Pawn or square that is difficult to defend.

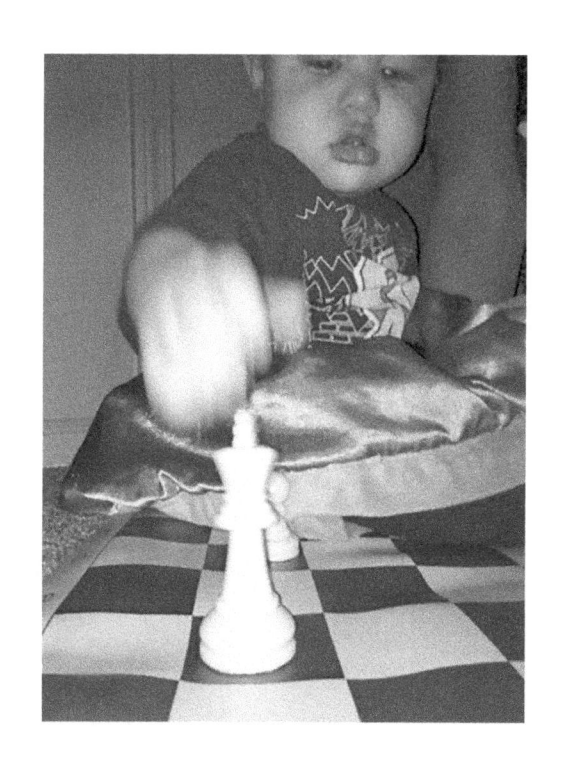

BLIND CHESS——25

Martha

Phil

ACKNOWLEDGMENTS

Enormous appreciation to the collective effort executed in the completion of this *Blind Chess* booklet. Exceptional thanks and applause to:

Martha Hoffman, her genius brought this to life and was everything;
Felicia Ann Smith, when all seemed lost because JAWS was gone, she saved the day,
Phil Sedgwick for his chess savvy and editing brilliance;
Brian Sweatt for his keen command of the English language and editing savvy;
Marc Molina for his friendship, tremendous support, and chess brilliance;
Quinn Burleson for his IT brilliance and chess savvy;
Dominique Andre Phifer for his Baby Boy love and support;
Loren Schmitt for his chess brilliance, wonderful support and kind heart;
Zeb Fortman for his extensive chess knowledge, chess master brilliance and executive editing; Zebfortman.com: Review his website for chess tutelage;
RJ Phifer II for his love, reading this booklet, patience, and support.

I love all of you for your contribution in helping to make my dream a reality.

God bless you.

Marc

Quinn

Randy

ABOUT THE AUTHOR

Born in Jamaica, New York, and educated in the public schools, I affectionately embraced math, sports, and chess with a competitive spirit at an early age. Learning the game of chess from my father at eight embedded a lifelong appreciation and fantasy for the game in my soul. The many times that we played gave me structure and foundation to navigate strategy in the development of my whole world. When you totally understand the game, an amazing relationship to everyday life unfolds. To share valuable hours absorbing wisdom from my father in that manner was simply priceless. That strategy is echoed and exhibited in the love extended from me to my sons and everyone I teach.

    Now that blindness and neuropathy are my reality, Blind Chess is the technique I use to play the game I love. Teaching others to play and enjoy this technique has become my passion.

    Contact my website www.Blindchess.net to facilitate and arrange a blind chess seminar to enlighten your staff, organization or group.

Lightning Source UK Ltd.
Milton Keynes UK
UKHW050822150621
385545UK00011B/624